THE FIRST SEASON

ADVENT CHRISTMAS EPIPHANY

Wayne Saffen

Fortress Press   Philadelphia

Library of Congress Catalog Card Number 73-79325

ISBN 0-8006-0166-1

Second Printing 1975

5329G75   Printed in U.S.A.   1-166

To my parents,
Earle and Opal Saffen

Their motto:
"To ease another's burden
is to forget one's own."

CONTENTS

THE violet hills ripen, waiting for snow to cover burnished flanks of brown and green, waiting to sprout newborn life when winter's day is done and spring begins.

So the round of the years cycles us through life attuned to nature's hues, immersing us in the colors of the seasons as aesthetic setting for our impression of things. The natural environment in which we live and move and have our being calls forth our first response to the wonder of everything that is. Those colors working on human sensibilities becoming aware of the shape and growth of things evoke that primal awe which develops into religious consciousness. They are new every day. Like swift changes in weather, they call forth our response to the world around us.

To this world we belong somehow, mysteriously, in spite of an unaccountable sense of alienation. Our alienation from Eden is the source of our feelings of estrangement, our religious awakening, and our search for reconciliation. We are "strangers in a strange land." We find ourselves at home as exiled residents.

Besides nature, there is also history. These two, nature and history, are intertwined as warp and woof of human life. In the midst of the green and gold, violet, white, and blue—all the hues of the techni-colored world—there surges forth blood, red from the arteries and veins of life, startling upon the landscape as it flows from their hidden courses. Blood is spilled upon the human scene in bright red obsceni-ties to mark the course of man and beast in pilgrimage to destinies unknown but dimly hoped for and brightly sought.

This, too, evokes a religious sense of awe and fear and wonder at the mystery and meaning of life, so pulsingly present in every moment, so tragically aborted in death. The tragedy of death arouses the tragic sense of life; we search for meaning in a world which is given but not explained. When murder is done and the carnage of war tears human communities, we object. We are not impressed by the argument that nature and history are violent by "nature," so that we should live in peace with violence as the natural order of things.

Violence impresses us not as natural but as crime. When human blood is shed, more than man is hurt. To kill human life is sensed as a crime against God, a thing to be answered for somewhere, sometime, somehow. Innocent suffering and death drive to the heart of anguish seeking expiation. Victorious shedding of blood is the story of history. "History is a butcher's bench." Blood is its "red badge of courage." Red is in every flag as guidon of a nation's glory.

Where innocent blood is shed, there God is found wounded in his Son, Jesus, and in all his suffering sons and daughters. It is God who redeems human life from destruction, forgives sins, and makes people whole again, liberating human beings from death for new life. The story of God in Christ, who despised not the shame of the cross, is the story of how God sacrificed himself for man. The tragedy of human existence is transformed into new and eternal life through resurrection.

The round of the church year tells this story annually. It meshes into the context of our own experience in our own time and place to shed meaning upon our own lives. *The first season* of the church year takes us from hopeful waiting to the appearance (Epiphany) of God in Jesus. Violet is the color of Advent. White is the color of celebration, at Christmas and Epiphany. *The second season* takes us from Lent through Ascension, focusing upon the trial and crucifixion of Jesus, his death and resurrection, and his return to God. The God-man Jesus sits now at God's right hand as legitimate ruler of the world, biding his time until he returns to complete his victory over all forces of evil and oppression for the final redemption of humanity from all enemies. In Christ, God sets life against death; he promises to deliver us from all demons, sin, death, and hell. Violet is the color of Lent. White is the color of Eastertide. *The third season* belongs to the Holy Spirit. The outpouring of the spirit of Christ into human beings sets the earth on fire with the vision of the kingdom of God. The church proclaims God's presence among men as King. Red is the color of Pentecost. The long green of summer is the season for the Holy Trinity of Creativity, Redemption, and Regeneration.

The church year is the story of God in human life, a sacred history which illumines profane history. It gives meaning to nature as the life-giving context of human existence in a sacramental universe. In a particularly felicitous phrase brought into consciousness by the ecological crisis, we are related and reconciled to our "life support systems."

Throughout the seasons red is designated for particular days, noting the martyrs whose "blood is the seed of the church," coming to terms with the fact that "without the shedding of blood there is no remission of sins." The church has not only a myth, its story, its religious interpretation of history. It has also its own history, sprinkled with blood—blood shed not for domination of man by empire and power but for the liberation of man through grace.

The following pages attempt to take us through the seasons of the church year in its colors and evocative moods by means of original poems, prose, and sermon to catch the feeling and meaning of our times. To go through a year in such a way, liturgically aware and responsive, is to sense life in its core meaning, to be reflective in the living of our days, to give ultimate and proximate meaning to all we experience and undergo as human beings.

The Bible is the great source book for this unexpected light on the human pilgrimage. The liturgical year is its rhythm. Nature and history are its contexts. Our time and place are its crucible for meaning.

In the hope that this reflective potpourri of prose, poetry, and pensées may prove illuminating and encouraging, we offer it to all who search for meaning in that human experience which questions us all. Jesus Christ is the Way, the Truth, and the Life. We may all return to the God and Father of us all who comes to us through him by the promptings of his Spirit who speaks to our innermost selves. Strange promptings of the Word stir us to uncalculated responses of faith, hope, and love of life. These are gifts of the Spirit who urges us to know God and receive life as gift and joy.

Manteca, California
Advent 1972

ADVENT

ADVENT

ADVENT is
  Waiting the last month
For the baby to be born.
Advent is
Waiting for the holidays.
Advent is
Waiting for something
To celebrate.
Advent is
Looking at the world
Through rose-colored glasses.

WAITING

WAITING is the hardest part.
We want to get going.
We want it to happen.
We want to get there.
We want to see how it turns out.
Waiting wasn't what we had in mind.

We spend our lives waiting:
Waiting for the train to come on time,
Waiting for calendar days
To fall to the floor,
Waiting to grow up,
Waiting to arrive,
Waiting to get away,
Waiting for somebody else
Who is never on time,
Or who is waiting, also, for others,
Waiting for the crisis to come,
Waiting for it to pass,
Waiting to get it into perspective historically
To see what it was that happened, really,
As if we needed something other
Than our experiencing selves to tell us.

Waiting for God, for Godot,
For whatever it is for which we wait,
Told patiently to stay in line—
And we wait patiently there, not sure why—
And in line we crane our necks
To see whether it is coming,
When and where.

We spend our lives waiting:
Waiting for the war to end,
Waiting for love to last,
Waiting for the End
To begin
What we have been
Waiting for
All our lives.

It's not the waiting
That's so hard.
It's not knowing
The time of appointment.

We need a definite time
To set our alarms for,
So we'll be ready.
But not too soon.

It's not the waiting
That gets us.
It's the indefiniteness
Of the time we're waiting for.
We have other things to do,
A set time, a lifetime,
To do them in.
We can't spend our whole lives
Waiting.

We know his tricks.
We're on to him.
He waits till we grow
Weary of waiting,
Then slips into history
Like some common infant
Born in any hovel every day,
Escaping our attention,
Diverted for the moment
To more important things.

He waits for a pregnant virgin
To deliver what we've been waiting for
While we were busy taking census,
Counting noses as if statistics
Were what really counted.

He slipped one over on us
That time. When we looked
To what was happening,
He disappeared
Into an ocean of infants
And took time to grow up.

WAITING FOR CHRISTMAS AGAIN

SO here we are waiting for Christmas again.
   It seems sort of silly after all these years
To go through the whole rigamarole again.
Christmas is coming. Santa is coming.
Jesus is coming. Children are coming.
Presents are coming. Bills are coming.

Canned music blares forth carols.
Store windows look like fairylands.
Countered goods go on credit cards
To be paid for when dates fall due.

So this is what Christmas has come to:
A crucial season in the national economy.
For this a babe was born in Bethlehem,
And poor unwanted children swarm the globe,
While favored children recite their verses
Before opening Christmas presents,
The real joy when Christmas duty's done.

Familiarity breeds contempt
And memorized miracles lose luster.

Christmas glow dissolves.
Fogs of sentiment dissipate
Into the commonplace of everyday.

"Christmas is for children,"
Say adults hardened by disappointments.
Nostalgia substitutes for wonder.
Christmas is a ghost of childhood past
Come to haunt the middle age of parentage.
Doting on our own children,
We are far, far away
From Bethlehem, from Harlem's slums,
From *favelas* and *barrios*
In Spanish America, from Saigon,
Calcutta, and Mozambique.

Christmas comes again this year.
It is coming, ready or not.
Christ is coming, ready or not.
He's newborn in slums, like it or not.
He's the one for whom we have no room,
Not then, not now, not ever,
Until we take his Advent
Seriously.

ADVENT? REPENT?

ADVENT? REPENT?

ADVENT? Repent?
For what?
For youth misspent?
For money lent?
Effervescence?
Obsolescence?
For dalliance
And misalliance?
For virgins *enceinte*
And *fils enfants*?
For tarried absence
Or harried presence?
For happenstance?
For nonchalance?
Relent, Advent.
We'll not repent.

Let Christmas come.
We're ready for it.
Mistletoe and holly scents,
Bourbon, scotch, and X-mas presents
Are not the flowers of repentance.
We're all spent, Advent.
Try again, in Lent.

PALM SUNDAY IN DECEMBER?

ADVENT 1
Matthew 21:1–9

CHRISTMAS in July?
June in January?
April bride and December groom?
Palm Sunday in December?
Happy New Year four Sundays before Christmas?
Do Christians always do things backwards,
Out of step, out of time, out of kilter, off beat?
So Janus looks both ways, backwards and forwards,
Retrospecting an old year, anticipating a new one.
What does the two-faced Roman god have to do with Jesus or us?
   Nothing.

Where is your orientation, anyhow?
How did you get so disoriented,
That you let lapse the liturgical year?

You let no other date lapse.
You know Christmas, because the culture primes you.
You remember birthdays and anniversaries.

You do not let insurance policies lapse.
You know when it's time to relicense your car.
The internal revenue deadline makes you sweat,
But you meet it.
You even know about July Fourth,
Though you may not have turned out for a parade
For a long time.

Why are you so surprised at this parade
Turned out for Christians four weeks before Christmas?
Why are you so surprised every year?
Don't you think you should have caught on by now?

Every parade marks a victory
And starts a procession towards the future.
On Palm Sunday you know what the parade's about.
Why are you so surprised to see it repeated now?
Is it just that you have stocked up on candles
And are all out of palm branches?
No, Christmas tree branches won't do.

Where do you think this journey to the manger is going?
Did you think it was all just about shepherds and magi?
Don't you know babies grow up?
Don't you know why we celebrate the birth of this one?

An ass bore Mary, pregnant, to Bethlehem from Nazareth.
An ass bore Mary and Jesus to Egypt. Joseph walked.
An ass bore Jesus into Jerusalem on Palm Sunday.

All babies are born to die,
Some to do great things along the way.
This baby-king is born to die to save and live again.
The ass knows the way.

AND THERE SHALL
BE SIGNS

ADVENT II
Luke 21:25–36

AND there shall be signs
In the sun and in the moon and in the stars.
And upon earth there shall be distress of nations
And much perplexity. The sea shall heave
And the waves' roaring shall scourge coastlands
With surging surf. Tidal waves shall rush inland

To snatch inhabitants from precarious perches.
Men's hearts shall fail for fear and dread,
Seeing and sensing the things that are coming
Upon the earth."

Advent is the sign these things are happening.
The whole world watches, waits for safe return
Of astronauts whose oxygen gives out rounding the moon.
Earthquakes shatter Andes mountains,
Rock ancient Iran, shake cities to rubble.
Tidal waves ride the vast Pacific looking for quarry.
Nations strut their military insanity,
Summoning men and hardware, inventing new causes
To unleash war's genocidal curse, distressing many
With seeming insolubility, perplexing those
Who think too much to just go along.
The worst is yet to come, we know, trying to forget
Nuclear-tipped missiles sitting underground in rural silos
Storing up the seeds of death for future generations,
Sterile seeds of demonic enterprise.

Think of this as you prepare to celebrate Christmas.
Christmas is not for forgetting this; it is for remembering,
And reminding, and keeping sharp in focus multi-possibled doom.
Bottled Christmas cheer for an alcoholic anesthesia

To drown all sorrows and anxieties in our tinseled paradise
Makes sense enough in man's suicidal poise above abyss.
It is not drunkenness that's sin so much as technocratic sobriety
Which acts as if it all made sense. Escape into oblivion
Is a defense mechanism to avoid the actuality of the void.
Do not prate about escapism, annihilators of men's hopes.
Do not criticize the way the wounded nurse themselves,
If you do not come with healing in your survival kit.

The consolation of nihilism, despair,
Mark of our time though it may be,
An apocalyptic mood so dark the sun is blotted out
In broad daylight for those transfixed by Nemesis,
Serves only to curtain hope which sees beyond,
Through the curtain, to a better day coming.
Fantasy and ecstasy envision worlds not yet seen
With empirical eyes. Faith says what can be envisioned
Can be hoped for beyond the dread.
Is Advent merely portent?

"And they shall see the Son of man
Coming in a cloud with power and great glory.
When these things begin to come to pass,
Then look up and lift up your heads.
For your redemption is drawing nigh."

Marvelous words, these.
There is nothing in the signs to show
This unprecedented hope is what is pointed to.
Beyond the curtain of oblivion, a threatened future
To be feared more than present misery,
Lies the promise of the second coming of the Son of man
In a cloud as bright as glory.

Like clouds which thunder darkly upon earth
Future's portent has a bright upper side turned to the sun.
Sons of men flying above the storm
Discover clouds are sunlit white.
The Son of man rides the clouds out into transcendence
Of circumstance, and God's face shines again on a darkling earth.
See the earth from the moon, son of man, what a fair planet it is,
Round and blue and brown and green swathed in white swirls.
Earth could be fair and air could breathe again, and will.
Mankind waits for redemption; the Son of man shall bring it.
He's out on the clouds now, winging his way in.
The transformation of mankind is only as far off
As the inside of the brain turned loveward
In hope that what can be will be, that all mankind can see
Redemption coming. It starts upon hearing this word
Of realizable hope. The Son of man is coming.
The sons of men need not repeat their fathers' mistakes.

J OHN the Baptist, in prison, is having second thoughts, serious doubts. He sends his disciples to ask Jesus if he is the one who is to come or if we should look for another. John's courage is not in question. It is his courage which landed him in jail. He preached repentance to all, to high and low. When he criticized the king for living with his brother's wife, that tore it. Such courage may be applauded after the fact, historically. But at the time it is reckoned folly, decidedly unsafe, both inside and outside churches. Criticism of those in authority is a subversive, seditious act, "bordering on treason," inspiring, as it does, disaffection and disloyalty in people, causing them to lose confidence in their government. Preachers will go to jail, or even be executed, if they do not watch their tongue. We saw Father Delp and Dietrich Bonhoeffer go to jail and die as martyrs in Nazi Germany. Now new names are added every day in the Americas.

Consider the case of the Berrigan brothers, and other priests and nuns, laymen and women, who protest against unjust war. When the Berrigans preached against war by burning draft cards and files instead of people, they were accused of "destroying government property." Napalm burning paper is a symbolic form of protest against napalm used for genocide against real men, women, and children in America's slaughterhouse in Asia. With due solemnity they were remanded to jail for the heinous crime of "destroying public property," a crime against the state. "Fugitives from injustice," as Daniel Berrigan put it, though pacifist, they were regarded as dan-

WHAT DID YOU GO OUT TO SEE?

ADVENT III
Matthew 11:2–10

gerous criminals to be taken forcibly with drawn guns. Such courage is surely folly in the eyes of most people. Nor is it better in prison where men of moral courage are set out for special treatment, not excluding homosexual assault. Their courage is not in question. Their manhood need not be proved. A more palpable and dangerous question presents itself in prison, in the quiet of their own minds. Were they really right? Could they have been wrong? How could they know for sure? When a man's truth is in question, the very basis on which he speaks and acts and risks is cast in doubt.

This was John's question. He had said and done all on the basis of his conviction that the kingdom of God was at hand, that Jesus would inaugurate it. John's task was to prepare people for this new kingdom, before which the kingdom of Herod or the Roman empire could hardly stand. God's prophet, he had the Word to wield against thrones, dominions, principalities, powers, spiritual wickedness in high places. He was God's mouth, God's voice, God's ax to cut at the root of human evil and sin, to chop at the tree of human hierarchy which grows in the soil of popular belief, obedience, and acquiescence. God's kingdom threatens all kingdoms when it comes in power, grace, and glory. No human artifice of statecraft can stand before it. Kings may well tremble on shaky thrones when people are summoned to the new order of things which will liberate them from old bondages. The prophet sees the new day coming. He will not likely see it come. He announces the vision. Then the turmoil begins, as the irresistible new is set against the recalcitrant old. He will pay in blood for his words as an agitator. His truth will vindicate him after his time. During his time he is a dangerous person who must be silenced. "Law and order" must be established and maintained against seditious speech which undermines people's allegiance to current political structures, the powers that be.

The kingdom of God will be tolerated if it is subsumed within the corporate structures of existing states. If it will not accommodate itself as support of existing institutions, it is posed as a threat, and must be dealt with as such. When he sets the new against the old, a man's courage is not at stake, although it will surely be tested. His truth is at stake. To be wrong about one's truth is not merely to be premature, untimely—it is to be fundamentally wrong in the perception of how things are and will be, to look without warrant for divine intervention. It is to entertain false hopes of a change in direction, to believe in possibilities of new vision which never materialize, and to cling to the illusion that fearless speech and creative action will help bring the new world into being. It is to pursue a fantasy head-on into a crash with reality which shatters everything.

The kingdom of God must be reality, if God be real. It must show up present social realities as unstable shams resting upon false premises and false promises. The establishment of injustice does not take kindly to dethronement and the establishment of justice. In a power-based world, words had better be backed with action, and action with superior power. The kingdom of God had better do with reality than with wish. Wishing won't make it so—at least not in the real world.

"What did you go out to see? A reed shaken by the wind?" This is what Jesus asked bystanders shocked by John's question. No, they did not come out to see a reed. They knew what they had come out to see, what everyone would come out to see: a strange man with long hair and wild beard (you know the hippie kind), dressed unsartorially in ragged skins, a rope around his waist. Like some sideshow geek, he ate locusts and honey. Uncouth, unmannered, nonconformist, different, strange. He preached to those who came to see him. He tore them apart for their establishment ways, for their hypocrisy. He did not just damn the system. He damned everybody. They loved it. It was the thing to do, to go out and hear him. It broke the monotony of ordinary days. Even scribes and Pharisees, and, of course, soldiers came. Always the scribes to get documentary evidence. Always the self-righteous to defend the national and religious honor and look for false prophets. And always the soldiers, in case the crowd got out of hand. They joined the chorus of questioners, blending into the curious, ambivalent, sometimes hostile crowd of curiosity seekers. "What should we soldiers do?" they asked. How should they repent? "Be satisfied with your wages and stop fighting among yourselves," John said. Smart aleck! He'd get his, sometime when they had him to themselves, after the crowds had gone. What he needed was to be taught a little respect for authority. But not now. Not when the whole crowd was watching. They were professionals. They retreated from their banter into their professional stance. John was no reed. But he would bend. Yes, he would bend. The man had not been born who could not be bent.

"What did you go out to see? A man clothed in soft raiment? Those kind live in king's houses," Jesus continued. Did they come out to see John model his latest fashions for men? Did they come out to see for themselves his shoddy dress, his unkempt appearance, his scraggly beard and all, to shake their heads at how fanatical religion and dropping out of straight society can unhinge a man and make him mad? Did they come out to feel superior and safe, to mark the fascinating deviant, to confirm their own social status proved by acceptable garb? "Don't go by appearances," suggests Jesus. People are always fooled by appearances. They make surface judgments. They think in categories and miss actual persons. Would they have listened to John any better if he had appeared in a business suit, neat and trimmed? Wouldn't they have said, if he occupied a respectable pulpit instead of mounting a desert rock, that his sermon was very good and they enjoyed it very much, not listening to what he said at all? Don't respectable people do just that, always?

"What did you go out to see? A prophet?" Who listens to prophets?

"I'll tell you what you really saw, what you came out to see and never saw at all because you were distracted by appearances and therefore mocked the man and his words. John was the greatest man ever born of woman." So what do you make of that? Could the greatest man who ever lived have appeared upon the human scene that way, in that place, dressed like that? He could and did, says Jesus. So what was it you think you came out to see? What attraction did this strange man in the desert have that drew crowds from their accustomed haunts to the desert to see him? What but curiosity would gather crowds? Repentance? Looking for the kingdom of God? Seeking truth? Try to mask curiosity, superiority, and snobbishness with religiosity and your hypocrisy will find you out.

"What did you go out to see? A reed, shaken by the wind?" Yes, a reed. A man is a reed, after all; even a strong man. The reed will bend before the wind. But it will not break. It must be broken. Men and reeds are broken every day, strong men and strong reeds. All flesh is grass. We are all reeds. But reeds do not try to break one another. Men do that. What God gives life to, men give death to. There must be satisfaction in breaking men and reeds. It is done so idly, so absent-mindedly, so deliberately. When men and reeds are broken, breakers and watchers-on look with surprised satisfaction at the fragility broken by their temporary exercise of power: "He (she, it) broke!" Then there are long philosophical and medical and psychiatric and managerial and military studies of stress on human beings, asking where the breaking point is. It is not enough to see a reed shaken by the wind, bending in grace before it. We must break it to demonstrate our power. It is not enough to see men bending before the winds of adversity, with grace and determination and resiliency. We must break them. There must be satisfaction in it, for we do it all the time. "What did you go out to see? A reed?" No. They went out to see how far the reed would bend before breaking.

Now the reed-man is in prison, awaiting death. He has remained unbent, unbroken in his adversity. But it looks as if he is going to break now, not outwardly but inwardly. What he has lived by is beginning to dry up. Soon he will become brittle enough to snap at the slightest pressure. It is his truth, held against all opposition and threat, which landed him in jail. If his truth is not true, he is wrong existentially. A man can die for truth, a martyr. But to die for nothing, to die for a case of mistaken identity, to be victim of one's own self-delusion, is tragic folly. So John asks his question and sends out disciples to find out for him. His question reveals that his inner truth remains unshaken. He does not doubt the kingdom of God will come. His question is one only of reassurance that Jesus is indeed the one for whom all have been looking for deliverance. Jesus would have to answer that for himself. What would be the signs that the kingdom of God comes with Jesus?

Jesus answers with a word for John, a word for the crowd, a word for us. "Go and show John again what you hear and see. The blind receive their sight, the lame walk, lepers are cleansed, the deaf hear, the dead are raised, and the poor have the Gospel preached to them. Blessed is he who shall not be offended in me." These are the signs. When the kingdom of God comes, that's the way it comes. Go tell John it is happening. Jesus does not promise to do it. He is doing it. Those who look for the kingdom of God can see for themselves whether it is happening. Where it is happening the kingdom of God breaks in upon man. Where it is not happening, no amount of religious talk can cover the absence of God. The failure of the church is evident in every failure to take these marks of the kingdom seriously and to substitute empty words for redemptive acts. Churches and church people are not serious about the kingdom of God unless they are serious about these things and see to it that they happen. Any serious seeker after the kingdom of God can see for himself where this is happening, whether the churches are serious about these things, and respond accordingly. The kingdom of God is where it's happening. All else is subterfuge and faithlessness.

Jesus has a word for the crowd, for those serious about the kingdom. They can now see John in a new light, as a messenger of God, a forerunner of the Messiah. John is the greatest man who ever lived. Nevertheless, whoever enters the kingdom of God from now on, great or small, will be greater than John. There it is. If men aspire to greatness, there is no higher calling. If men seek the kingdom of God, it will be found where God's power is at work healing the sick, the halt, the maimed, the blind, the deaf and dumb, where encouragement is given to the poor to release them from their bondage of oppression. This is such good news that when it happens it cannot be suppressed or silenced. Human redemption is coming! It is near! It is here! That is the message of Advent. John is God's messenger. Jesus is our Redeemer. We are his disciples.

"So, what did you go out in the desert to see?"

Or, to put it another way, why did you come to church today?

VOICE IN THE WILDERNESS

ADVENT IV
John 1:19–23

WHEN a voice cries in the wilderness,
Seemingly to empty rocks and sand and brush,
People come to see what it's all about.
When a voice cries in the city,
It is just one more noise in the ceaseless pain.
It is absorbed, diffused, entered into the record
Of indifference. The city's cry, unheeded,
Turns to violence and fire in desperate bid
For attention.

In the wilderness the voice rings out crisp,
Staccato sound not belonging to that place,
Ricocheted on echoing rocks,
Swallowed up by vastness' silence.
Undistracted ears hear its singular clarity.
The city is a wilderness of man-hewn rocks in neat array,
Green grass and broken-bottled lawn,
Conduits mazed underground.

Its natural inhabitants scurry like squirrels
Intent upon hoarding in security's mad scramble.
Human animals caged in office, school, and home
Go beetle-armored through the streets
On civilized rubber tires thinking uncivilized thoughts.
Voices are tuned in and out on radio and television
And cocktail conversations, as befits the mood.
Nothing serious intrudes. The place for preachers
Is off the streets in buildings set aside for irrelevance.
The ordinary cacophony must not be distracted by transcendence.

The wilderness is the place to go to see and hear.
It speaks its own language of silent witness.
Rocks imposed by time, hot sands to wear sandals in,
Air so clean and sun so bright they summon to awareness
In an alien place. No signs of comfortable familiarity here.
Only actualities to reckon with to survive.
The solitary man comes to hear the unspoken word
And becomes a prophet of what he's seen and heard in nature's wild
To fastidious men drawn out of urban shells to risk exposure.

The way of the Lord will be made straight first in the wilderness,
Where property values and vested interests do not prohibit.
Mountains and hills gouged through by bulldozers cutting concrete
    tracks

And valleys upgraded into roadway connect cities of hill and plain,
Where men drive back and forth oblivious, preferably at night,
Because (they say) there's nothing there, it's all empty,
Until unsettled times and urban plight drive new nomads
Into desert hippie havens, charmed by the barren stretches
And sheltering mountains, uncontaminated yet by land developers.
New voices in the wilderness cry silently of civilization
And its discontents, preaching repentance and practicing
What they preach. They draw, as usual for phenomena,
New human hordes to see why they're there. Human beings
Are made straight again in wilderness, going forth into
Strange new lands (inside/outside) to be discovered.
Huddling together there they recover lost community.
It is their own hills and mountains, expectations of achievement,
Which are leveled to more realistic and primal scales of values.
Desert survival training schools teach what social engineering
For upward social mobility cannot know about life and meaning.
Our own valleys of despair, despond, must be raised
To higher elevations, above depression, above the fear of failure,
Above the mock charades demanding men to play deadly games
Of emptiness if they would live. The highway goes
Through the desert to such new folk. Throngs come
To see and hear those who are on the track of the Answer
And the Way.

CHRISTMAS

WHILE
MEN
SLEEP

G OD gives
To His beloved
In sleep."

The earth turns.
Night falls.
Day dawns.
Stars form.
Cells multiply.
Dew glistens.
Atmosphere condenses.
Seeds germinate.
Plants grow.
Trees bud.
Flowers open.
Grain matures.

*Published in the *Lutheran Witness Reporter,* December 1969, p. 13.

The sleeper
Sleeps on.
The Creator
Renews.

In silence a star
Looks from afar
Almost unnoticed.
The Son of God
In natal quiet
Takes on humanity.

Bethlehem sleeps.
Jerusalem sleeps.
Rome sleeps.
A world sleeps.

But Mary does not.
Joseph does not.
Shepherds do not.
God does not sleep.

He gives
All unawares,
In spite

Of human fears:
Daily food,
Precious blood,
Mother to child,
Life to life.

A Son He gives.
In flesh He gives.
Spirit He gives.
Salvation He gives.

While men sleep on,
While the earth turns,
While only watchers wake,
And only wakers watch.

PEACE ON EARTH
GOOD WILL TO MEN

WHAT we all
   Hope for, pray for, fight for,
Kill for, live for, despair of,
Comes as a gift.

It is not to be won at all.
No war can win it.
Peace is when the war is over.
War requires enmity to win,
Not good will.

Good will is for peacemakers,
God's children.
It is God's gift.

Why do we love our Christmas so,
If it is not the news,
The good news,
The very best of good news,
That God brings peace to earth,
That good is what God wills for man?

CHRISTMAS DAY
Luke 2:8–14

What is the meaning of a baby?
Any baby, yours or mine,
Ourselves once, too.

Once there was
When we were not at war
With any one.
We were too young
To know who enemies were.
All our fears were nameless.
All men were friends to us, we thought.
Openness and trust
Were in our beaming faces.
A childlike faith we had.
It was all true.
God loved us, this we knew,
For the Bible told us so.
And fathers did, and mothers, too.

Since then we have become educated.
We have found what men can do
When fear and hate tear at the heart.
We have learned to growl ourselves
At others, weaker, who incur
Our momentary displeasure.

We have our wars to prove our courage
And pray for peace we will not keep when given
For fear we shall be thought cowards.
Suspicion replaces good will, and
Competition turns all men into enemies.
We may not be good—that's optional—
But we must be better, best of men.
We must excel in supremacy,
Mark of successful men.

So we come to Christmas
To weep awhile at what might have been.
We grow romantic, pastoral, bucolic, maudlin.
We think of rolling hills and shepherds
Watching sheep by night and playing flutes
Beside a flickering fire. When angels come,
They know where to go. Where else, except
Where the setting lies peaceful and serene,
Undisturbed by distant thunder of men at war,
Night sky broken only by the swift arc of a jet plane
Threading the stars, going home somewhere?
A whole host of glory could break upon such a night,
At such a sight as men at peace with others and themselves.

Only intrusion would rouse latent fears,
Set shepherds on their guard,

Perk up dog's ears, set nostrils aquiver.
"Fear not!" would be the thing to say to shepherds
Armed for wolves and predators.

Good news to men was brought first to men
Who were themselves at peace.
Good will to man is willed to men
Predisposed to ways of peace,
Whom God has made already willing.

They can see the baby first.
They will not harm it.
They will understand it.
They will know what to say
About what they see.

The rest of us?
We come only to listen,
Charmed by the alien scene,
Wishing it were so,
Taking a night off for fantasy
(Fearing its reality)
Before going back to the office
Or to another war.

CHRISTMAS TV SPECIAL

"RING AROUND THE MOON"

(unless scratched)

AND so to winter's cold imaginings.
Electric light and heat and TV tube
Encapsulate another world like none
Outside the walls. Reality recedes
To haunt the great outdoors for wintry
Postcards sent from Florida. Wish
You were here and all that. While
Santa looks for chimneys to drop in
On which don't land him in the
Furnace. And reindeer have more horse-
Power this year, all eight of them,
Driving cleated tires over ice-crested
Snow from storms which came too early
For a Bing Crosby Christmas, sooted
Down, urban style, for another bleak
Black Christmas (not Jesse Jackson's
Kind). And people went to church (they

Really did) to hear children sing 'round
Aluminum Christmas trees, fireproofed to
Guard every plastic baby jesus; while
Real babies cried in ghetto hideaways,
Herod-haunted (and mothers, too; and
Raging, helpless fathers), because hymn-
Singing and caroling Christian taxpayers
Don't really want all those damned babies
In ADC cribs. Mary's going to get it
From the legislature this year. People
Are fed up with all that Christmas overstock
Of infant flesh. Who ordered it all,
Anyhow? We wish you a merry Christmas,
And a happy New Year. Jesus Christ!
Man in space! What will they think of
Next? So God became man. So what? Our
Eyes are on the stars. You know what
We're aiming for. Ring around the moon!
How's that, Old Man? You ain't seen
Nothin' yet. And it's all on television.
And so to winter's cold imaginings. . . .
[Repeat till sign-off. Save tapes for
Reruns next summer. They'll go great
With beer and keep restless natives off
Streets to watch Man's All-Seeing Eye.]

KILL THE WITNESS

ST. STEPHEN, MARTYR
Acts 6–7
Matthew 23:34–39

THREE days huddle next to Christmas,
    Coming afterward in swift succession, strangely placed.

St. Stephen's Day is first.
Our first Christian martyr was stoned to death for a sermon.
It is not a Christmas story, but it is what happens, sometimes.
Taking Jesus seriously has been known to get men killed.
Stephen was a deacon. He helped people, widows, orphans, needy
    folk.
He was full of faith and power and did great wonders among people,
The record says. He taught with remarkable wisdom. And he had
A great spirit, so we're told. An altogether lovely person.
The kind of person who inspires love because he gives it.
The kind of person everybody likes because he's good. Except some.
There are always some to whom excellence in others
Is a personal affront. Christlike, loving persons
Are often destroyed to give evil men peace and satisfaction.

Stephen won his religious arguments against opponents.
Argument failing, a different strategy was devised to deal with him.
Watch closely; the method never varies. They suborned men
To bear false witness against him, to assassinate his character,
To charge him publicly with heresy, to undermine his credibility,
To prejudice the populace against him.

"We heard him speak blasphemous words against Moses
And against God, against the temple, against the Law.
We have heard him say that Jesus of Nazareth will destroy
This place and change the customs which Moses handed down to us."

Get the picture? Notice the familiar, stereotyped charges:
Blasphemy against our religion, against God, temple, law,
Inciting to riot, threatening destruction, changing customs.
Substitute freely the sacred cows and shibboleths of any society.
The charges are not true, of course. They need not be,
Are not meant to be. Truth is not their function.
How does one defend himself against all of them at once?
Stephen countered with a sermon, public preaching at its best:
You killed the Lord of Life as your fathers killed the prophets.
It was a great sermon, all true. It got Stephen killed.
They took him outside the city and stoned him to death. Why?
Because he told the truth publicly about what happened to Jesus.
He hurled the truth in the face of public authorities

Trying to cover up official crime, official murder.
Undaunted by one murder, the authorities pursued others.
Determined to break up the movement, they moved with unmitigated
Zeal to break up its leadership. Sound familiar?

The second day after Christmas belongs to Saint John the Divine.
Jesus' closest friend among the disciples saw too clearly
And knew too much to be left at large. The same kind of
Authorities who keep the peace of injustice with laws
Invented for occasion exiled him.
Repressive "order" preserves society from truth's agitation.
A witness to truth is martyr always.
John was not murdered, like Stephen, to close his mouth.
He was only exiled,
Sent far enough away to remove his infectious presence,
To prevent the plague of truth from spreading,
To prevent God's peace from breaking out everywhere.
It was no victory for tyrants, power mad myopics.
Exiles write books that keep the movement going,
Inspired words to set against the intransigence of old orders.
If speakers are dangerous enough to kill for what they say,
Writers are even more dangerous, for they set words in print,
Write the records of what really happened,
Demolishing official versions of political purge.
Persecuted books survive, underground if necessary, thrive,

Until the movement wins its day.
Then they are canonized as new authorities,
Guarded by new defenders of the faith, who miss their point,
And launch new inquisitions.

The third day after Christmas belongs to Holy Innocents,
Slaughtered innocents, massacred, caught unawares
In Herod's storm of rage against the Prince of Peace
Who had the temerity to be born in his jurisdiction.

All this makes for a very bloody Christmas,
As if the day itself were but a lovely truce
In the middle of a war, where enemies stop shooting
For a day to be sentimental in, and sane,
To celebrate what they say all their wars are fought for:
Peace on earth! Good will among men!

We protest that all our wars are prosecuted
For a just peace, not simply for victory,
Winnable if only our enemies would give up their intractability,
And obey us in their own countries where we have come
To impose our version of peace upon them.
We will have our just peace in their world,
No matter how long the war must go on, no matter
How much blood and money it takes, theirs and ours.

No sacrifice is too great to assure our dominance.
So it goes with men and nations seeking peace through war.

Each Christmas breaks into the bloody mess,
Charms us out of sight
When confronted with sheer innocence.
Each Christmas we say we wish
The Christmas mood could last the year around—
And wonder why it doesn't.
We shake our heads at foolish men
And go back to killing each other
The very next day.

Christmas is not a mood, of course.
It is a fact dropped into history.
Its actuality engenders wistful moods in us,
Opens awareness of what could be,
Wishes that are not impossible dreams,
Realities that can be realized, and have been,
Hopes that can be fulfilled because they are possible
Christmas is not the impossible dream.
It is its very possibility that startles us,
Draws us to it,
Starts a new time clock going in history,
Replacing ancient cycles of revenge.

It is only our sin
Which cheats our dream of peace from fulfillment.
Something can be done about that.
Christmas is the start of the story
Of what God will do about that.

Our problem is not with Christmas—
That's real enough—but with us.
It's our moods that change,
Our reverie that's broken by reality.
Jesus was not born into a dream world
But a real one. He didn't live
In a dream world either.
Nor can we.

It is because Christmas deals with reality,
That Christians remember the very next day
The first martyr who bore our own new name of "Christian."
Real Christians risk getting persecuted, killed,
For trying to turn the world upside down,
Diverting men from ways of war to peace
With God and man through Christ.

New blood of innocence, good blood,
Is added to the old, bad blood of reprisal

Staining the habitat of man grown furious
At witnesses living against him,
Whose life styles and free speech
Bring his own self-righteous behavior
Under judgment.

Christmas is good news.
God makes peace with men
By forgiving them.
The Prince of Peace demonstrates
The seriousness of his intent,
His steadfast will.
He will insist upon it.
His peace shall prevail.
All our killing cannot stop
The Lord and Giver of life.
We are not quite ready for it.
Our war with God and man goes on.
So after every Christmas Stephen dies again—
But not unremembered,
Not without marring our Christmas mood,
Not without sustaining the witness he died for,
Not without God's vindication,
Who calls out such men from among us
In every age.

LOVE IS WHAT IT'S ALL ABOUT

ST. JOHN,
APOSTLE, EVANGELIST
John 21:19–24

THE thing is faith, said Paul.
   The thing is hope, said Peter.
The thing is work, said James.
The thing is love, said John.
Love is what it's all about.

Some son of thunder he,
To settle for love in a man's world,
Where faith looks for things unseen,
Courage tries for them against all odds,
And work sets hands to achieve them.

John speaks in a woman's voice
Of things soft and pliable and yielding.
Love is not a man's word.
Lust is. Sex is. Ambition is.
A religion of love is for women and children
And long-haired dropouts from society
Who couldn't do a day's work if they had to.
Or so we think.

What if God were love, as John says he is?
What if God loved the whole world?
What if Jesus died for love of humankind?
What if he were not simply victim and hater of oppressors?
What if love's sacrifice is the saving thing?
What if love is stronger than death?
What if love is greater even than faith or hope?
What if love never fails and lasts forever?
St. Paul admitted that.

If love were the chief thing in life,
We could believe all things, hope all things, endure all things.
Love would be at the heart of everything that counts.

Paul was true to his faith, and was killed for it.
Peter was courageous to the end, to the point of crucifixion.
James worked himself to death preaching Christ to assassins.
John lived to be a very old man, not at all bitter at the end,
Looking forward to what he had already seen in visions.

To know that love is at the core of life
Is to know life and live to love.
To know that love is life and life is love
Is to know what it's all about.

We remember John at Christmas because
He told us what it's all about.
Christmas is about God's love for humankind in Jesus Christ.
God loved the world so much
He gave his only Son for everyone,
That not one should perish,
That all may have eternal life
Through faith in him.
God did not send his Son into the world to condemn the world.
Listen, world, do not be so proud about your damnation!
It is one thing to reject a rejecting God.
It is quite another to spit in the face of salvation.
Do you love your misery so you will not give it up for love?
God sent his Son into the world
That the world might be saved by him, through him, in him.
That's love! That's life! That's what it's all about!

Jesus said many things and did many things
Which never got in books, said John, Jesus' friend.
Do you want to know about those things? Why?
What is written is enough.
Come to terms with what is written first.
You are not ready yet for what is not written.
What you yourself will write depends on what you read from Writ.
What is writ is given to kindle faith,

That we might believe that Jesus is the Son of God
(And more than that, that we are God's children, too).
Believing that, we have eternal life.
What more do you want?
To love and be loved is to come alive at last,
To stay alive as long as we live, and then some.
The thing of it is, we discover it so late!
It's good to see it newborn in a crib for everyone.
Love is what it's all about.
Love came down at Christmas
And was born anew in human hearts.

THE MURDER OF INNOCENCE

THE HOLY INNOCENTS
Matthew 2:13–18

WHY would soldiers do a thing like that?
How could grown men with automatic weapons in hand
Kill defenseless men, women, and children,
Whose only crime was being there

Where they lived in their own homes?
How could grown men drop napalm on playing children,
Innocence incinerated not in hatred but with unfeeling disregard?
How could infants threaten brave warriors of land and sky?
What threat do they pose to distant monarchs
Who play with men's destinies as poseurs at freedom
And purveyors of overkill?

Herod's men took sword in hand,
Hacked little children to bloody stumps,
Upon the mere command of a vassal king,
Hoping to catch in some captured Jesus some incipient guerrilla
Hiding in pink baby flesh, biding his time to strike.
Herod's stroke is preemptive.
Babies who do not grow up
Cannot become guerrilla threats to illicit thrones.
Ask any soldier. He will tell you why babies must die.
"They will grow up and become men,"
Say killers of My Lai and Bethlehem.
The murder of innocents innoculates the guilty
Against the threat of their survival.
Commanders must protect their men
Against the triumph of innocence.
The living must be sought to join the dead,
Lest life prevail and death forfeit suzerainty.

What throne is so mighty
That it can't be toppled by a mere infant
Left to grow to manhood without a murdered innocence?
If the child survives the massacre, somehow, miraculously,
There is always the cross to handle future contingencies,
To punish those who will not give up their innocence.

Do you really think so, Herod, Caiaphas, Pilate, Caesar?
You lost the fight the day you drew your sword
And dispatched your bombers to kill *enfants terribles*.
You know you cannot stem the tide of life and hope
Until you dare the "final solution to the human problem."
You know that genocide is on your mind and that you lost
When you settled for half measures.
You know that Christ will slip your net.
You knew before you started.
You know you've lost.
So why don't you give it up?
When Christ is risen,
Only you are not surprised.

TIME TO GO, OLD MAN

AN old man doesn't want to go any more than anyone else,
Unless he is wearied of life and everything becomes a burden
Too great to be borne any more. There are still things left
To see and do, and one hates to leave before the drama ends.
Old men hang on by the skin of their teeth
In privileged sanctuaries of seniority in congress and church
And elsewhere where reins of power and prestige are held
In gnarled but very firm hands
Until retirement forces them to the sidelines.

For an old man to hold a child in his arms
Is to see himself beginning all over again in another,
To know that what eludes the grasp can still be clutched at,
That each new generation holds the promise
Of redeeming the failures of the past.

An old man who has nothing left to do but wait
Must find a place to sit and watch for some last revelation,
On a park bench or in front of the TV.
He scans the daily news with seasoned eye, noticing repetitions,
Shaking his head at all the tumultuous new,
Too strange to adjust to.

Simeon waited in the temple.
Every new baby was brought there, sooner or later.
The one for whom all were waiting would show up in due time.
Simeon did not wait for his own revelation.
He was waiting for the consolation of Israel.
He was a very special kind of man, just and devout.
It was said the Holy Spirit was upon him.
When he saw the baby Jesus,
He took him up in his arms and blessed God.
Now he could depart in peace,
For he had seen God's salvation
Prepared before the face of all people
In this infant flesh.
He would enlighten Gentiles
And glorify God's people, Israel.

What did Simeon see?
What could he see but a baby?
What hopes are there in children
That old men are willing at last to depart in peace
And leave the salvation of the world to younger hands?
What in youth can stir such hope in age?
It is not youth itself but what God can do with it.
It is not just any baby who will make the difference,
But this one when he comes to do what he will,

When he grows up and really does it.
To recognize the promise and to trust fulfillment
Is to trust the future in such a way
That old age can let go of the past
For the better yet that God will do.

But there are warnings, too.
Pain will come, and parents must be ready for it,
When the child who makes them happy now
Sets out on his adult course.
"This child shall be set for the fall and rising of many in Israel,
And for a sign that shall be spoken against.
A sword shall pierce your own soul.
The thoughts of many hearts will be revealed
When they encounter your son."

How disruptive a savior this one will be!
Because of him many will fall from places of preeminence, domi-
    nance.
It is not simply that he comes and is accepted
And occupies the slot prepared for him in the going system.
The system itself will be disrupted and rearranged.
Another set of values will give men rank and place.
As many will fall, so also many will rise through him:
Casualties of life, victims of oppression, neglected ones,

Outcast for all the usual reasons from straight society,
The first shall be last and the last shall be first.

What mother would not have her heart pierced
By what would happen to her son when grown into major conflict?
She would not always understand him herself.
Was he just some troublemaker who made it hard on everyone,
Who didn't fit in but agitated for unwelcome change?
Was he really just some common criminal
To be disposed of finally as incorrigible
On some lonely hill of crucifixion, execution,
Mocked by the superiority-conscious crowd
Which always crows at weakness impaled in helplessness?

What thoughts of envy, pride, would not be revealed
When hatred and lies nail the vulnerable truth to the cross?
When salvation comes it exposes hearts for what they are.
How we react to Christ is how we fall from pride or rise from despair.
The cross illumines life. It shows where everyone is.
Christ's light shines out to penetrate nations.
Jesus is a sign to be spoken against when times are changing.
For an old man to hold this child in his arms,
It is enough to see what he will bring to the future
In a world in need of consolation and of hope.

THE NAME
CUTS DEEP

THE NAME OF JESUS
Luke 2:21

HERE'S another one.
　　A boy, eight days old.
It's time: time to cut away
Unneeded flesh, to sign the scar
Of God in manchild's private place.
No one else will know but him and his.

The rite calls for a name.
Have you a name yet, son?
What shall we call you, little giant?
Call his name "Jesus"? Why?
Because he'll save his people?
What a huge load for such little shoulders.
What dreams parents have, what expectancies.
Poor little child, to have God's work
Assigned so soon.

Cut the name in deep.
Tattoo it indelibly on tortured Hebrew flesh.
Scar it with raw wounds to acquaint you early
With cross and barbs and nail.
You'll be Jew soon enough to know
The Name cuts deep in certain flesh.
Now you belong to God.
There's no escaping that.
His name is yours for eternity.
Get used to it now.
"Jesus" is the handle you'll get used by.
You'll wish you could change your name
Into incognito, when the whole world
Calls it out in curse and prayer.

Go home for now, lacerated boy.
Don't grow up too soon.

A YEAR LIKE THIS
WINNOWS ONE

A YEAR like this winnows one.
What hurricane of hate
Roared through all the world
To shake the tree of life?
Strong men fell, violently wrenched
From green-leaved boughs ere Autumn came
To sear the leaf and loosen stems waving
To the westerlies. Too soon they fell,
Not from old age, overripe,
At harvesting's full maturity,
But greening, developing, before their prime,
The hardness of youth still in them,
The spirit not yet spent, not yet succumbed
To *ennui*. Old adages proved true (for
Whatever comfort to conservatives).
"The good die young." Indeed, they do.
Fine young men, black and white and brown
(And yellow, too) reddened Vietnam
With life's unracial, common blood,
To appease ungodly gods, impassive potentates
In Washington, and God knows where.

Ubiquitous presences of superpower dispense
Fatalism in computed doses of fatalities
Till all the odds are even, or eliminated.
Whom these gods would make mad, they first
Destroy. Destruction has become our commonplace.
Only protestors seem different, unfit for clean society.
The good die young, who seek a newer world.
RFK: 42-22-6/6/68—"Tell us not in mournful
Numbers life is but an empty dream." Where,
Then, the dream of him who dreamed a dream
Of black and white together? Martin Luther
King! There was a name to conjure with.
He died for garbagemen, to be better paid.
He could not pay better than with his life
In Memphis, Tennessee. And Old Man River,
He didn't say nothing. He just kept rolling
Along. The good die young. And "nice guys
Finish last." So passed Norman Thomas
From this vale of fears, fearlessly,
Perpetual loser who never made president
In six tries, but won his points nonetheless.
What more could you ask of an old Socialist?
He did his part. Do we ours? And Karl Barth,
John Steinbeck, Thomas Merton. These lovely
People, where do they all come from?

FLIGHT
TO
EGYPT

L ONG before Israeli fighter bombers
Flew deadly runs over Egypt,
Updating Middle Eastern continuing quarrels
From centuries of war and conflict,
Jews fled to Egypt for safety.
There have been peaceful interludes
When humanness prevailed.

When Herod murdered innocents in Bethlehem
Searching in vain for an infant Jesus,
Joseph headed for friendlier territory.
When famine comes, or war or persecution,
Jews head for the Nile.

Jesus was born where politics directed.
He began his life as a political refugee.
He ended it executed as a political criminal.
Jesus was in politics from start to finish.

Whoever says religion and politics don't mix
Has little knowledge of their historic conflict.
Both lay claim to rule the life of men.
God and Caesar never were at peace, never will be.
Nor are their subjects. Their claims compete
For allegiance of people caught in a schizoid bind.
Herod, not to be outdone by Caesar,
Had his own bloody ax to grind against God
In the face of the helpless poor in his own bailiwick.
Joseph and Mary must flee to Egypt with Jesus
Until there is a change in administration.
When Herod is dead a growing boy
May be safe from royal wrath for a while.
A man may stand and fight or run away.
It is a strategic decision which to do and when.
When children are targets in the war of the old against the young,
A man tries to do the best by his family.
There must be a safe place for them till madness is over.

Even so, one returns from exile cautiously.

Joseph had a dream in Egypt
That Herod had died in Judea.
An angel of the Lord appeared in his dream

Saying it was safe to return.
Politicians aren't seeking young people's lives any more.

Whatever anxiety is on one's mind
One is likely to dream about it.
The meaning of Herod's death for them
Is worked out in the night's dreamwork.
Yes, dreams are wishes.
Yes, Joseph wanted Herod dead, prayed him dead.
God answers such prayers, do not doubt it.
Whoever kills children to keep his throne
Has chosen God as his enemy.

Jesus is only one of many refugees
Seeking safety in exile.
Joseph is not the only father
To seek a safer place for his children
Where they can grow up alive and well.
In peace and war, God's sons commute.

EPIPHANY

WISE MEN
AND
EPIPHANY

WISE men do not always come from the East.
  Nor do they always follow stars.
But they do cross boundaries
And pay attention to what is happening
In the rest of the world.

What would flag-waving chauvinists know
About what happens beyond national boundaries,
Unless some battle call sets jingoist blood to boil
In patriotic fervor to murder utter strangers overseas
And assault informed dissenters at home?
Chauvinists have no time for intellectuals,
For stargazers or bookworms,
For historians or poets or philosophers.
And kings are much too busy keeping order
To watch out for the hidden springs of things
Which erupt to make history unmanageable, unaccountable.

Wise men who act upon a hunch or follow stars
Are rare in our technological, regulated world.
Scientific temper leads men to follow stars
In their heavenly courses with practiced eye,
To track the atoms in their trackless places,
To let hypotheses lead to their conclusions,
And test to see how it all turns out.

Let those whom nature teaches show the way
To blind historicists and administration scribes.
Let research scholars and scientists confer.
Let them check each other's data, books, observations.
Phenomena new in discovery may be old in the record.

Epiphany is revelation.
Things hidden in plain sight are made manifest,
Unobserved except by those with eyes trained to see.

For Zoroastrian magi, priest magicians,
Wise men, scientists in a prescientific age,
To bring gold and frankincense and myrrh
For a king born in obscurity noted only by natal star
Is an act of faith that stars do not mislead,
That signs in the heavens can be counted on
To enlighten earthlings whose calendars expect events.

How embarrassing to native born
That foreigners should know significant events
In our own land, which escape us.
If foreigners can know more than we,
If they are not at all inferior because different,
How can our assumed supremacy prevail?
How could they know our new leaders before we do?
Our books must be better than their stars,
Our scribes more intelligent than their scientists,
Or our national preeminence, based on the presumption
Of our superior intelligence, will be imperiled.

Scientists smile.
Science knows no national boundaries,
Nor does intellect.
The community of knowledge cannot be sundered
By dotted lines on maps.
Nor do sun or satellite stop at boundary checkpoints
Displaying proper visas to let them pass.

The mind is for searching mysteries,
Eyes are for watching stars, for careful observation,
And man is for everyplace that God creates a home.

When Jesus is born in Bethlehem, magi, foreigners,
Are first to know something significant has happened.

When the next new galaxy is discovered,
The man on the street will be checking ball scores,
Economists will have their eyes fixed on GNP and balance of payments,
Militarists will push their arms race towards Armageddon,
Gathering intelligence on potential enemies
They multiply themselves in self-fulfilling prophecies,
While presidents and their advisors
Go through motions of diplomatic protocol.

Even now those who are to be kings on earth
A generation hence are hidden among us, unrecognized.
We know not their names or time or place.
There is no natural order of succession.
God stores up his own surprises in hamlets,
In all the hovels of history.
When Messiah comes, stars will know. Magi, too.
But Herod will not know,
And his scribes will be caught napping.

When Christ comes again
Must Christians, too,
Wait for strangers to tell us?
Must each Epiphany come as a surprise
Because we weren't watching?

A CONFLICT OF AUTHORITY

JESUS was not a child prodigy
   Who did his one thing exceptionally well.
He did his one thing better than most,
But he also grew up balanced.

EPIPHANY I
Luke 2:41–52

After twelve years
His parents knew what to expect of him.
He was dependable and obedient.
They could trust him out of their sight for a whole day,
As long as they knew where he was.

Then at twelve a break in the pattern? Disobedience?
A betrayal of expectations?
After looking for him in panic for three days,
They found him in the temple at Jerusalem,
Sitting among teachers, asking questions.

A boy wants to know what a man is.
A boy wants to know who God is.
He wants to know why people die,
Why God lets it happen.
He wants to know what sin is,
Why it makes God and parents and other authorities so angry.

He wants to know what is in the books, sacred ones and others.
He wants to know what the temple's for,
What it has to do with life in the everyday world,
Why all the animals are killed there,
Why blood is sprinkled all over the place.
He also wants to know why people kill each other in wars.
He wants to know why his country is occupied by a foreign power,
Why soldiers walk his streets as if they owned them,
Why bigger brothers go overseas to fight.
He wants to know what's inside the Holy of Holies,
Why he can't go inside the secret sanctuary,
And what's with it with the incense.
He wants to know what all the rules and regulations,
Laws and commandments, prohibitions and taboos are for.
He wants to know who he is, what God expects of him.
A twelve-year-old boy is full of all sorts of questions
Just waiting for a teacher who really knows the answers.

Precocious? Perhaps.
Such precocity is to be found among most twelve-year-olds
Whose curiosity has not been blunted by those who suppress ques-
    tions
And make children feel guilty and foolish for asking.
Whatever dams and stops and inhibits
All the really important questions

Violates the soul of man and child.
The questions a man bears in his mind a whole lifetime
Belong to life and meaning and destiny.
God himself places questions there
By facing man with the enigma of his own existence.
Man's religious quest is prompted by God's Spirit.

Jesus' parents interrupted this supremely important search
With a comparatively unimportant one of their own.
They had not the wit to see what was going on,
Blinded by their own concerns and worries.
Like most parents, they put a parental stop
To what the boy thought was important.

"Son, why have you treated us like this?
Your father and I (to double the authority,
Inculcate guilt) have been looking all over for you,
Worrying half to death for fear and sorrow
Of what might have happened to you."

What's a twelve-year-old boy to say to that?
How thoughtless and inconsiderate he must have been
To have worried them so.
But wasn't the truth of it that he hadn't asked,
Because he feared (or knew) they would say no?

The spirit of a twelve-year-old
Is not broken so easily.
He is not to be just an obedient child,
Completely subject to the will of others, even parents.
He has a mind of his own,
A life of his own to develop.
His ways will not be their ways.
Parents must understand that.

"How is it that you sought me?
Did you not know
I would be in my Father's house,
About my Father's business?"

The claims collide.
An identity is formed and staked out.
Children do not belong to parents.
Children belong to God.
They belong to themselves.
People do not own people.
Parents do not always understand this,
So children must tell them.
Parents should remember
That once they had to tell their own parents
The same thing.

The new understanding was negotiated silently,
But decisively and clearly.
The confrontation was over.
Each had had his say.
Each was different afterward.
A change had occurred which was irreversible.
A new consciousness was born,
A new authority realized.
There is an authority beyond that of parents or state.
God is the ultimate authority,
The Father whose business true sons attend to.
That business has priority over all others,
And his house is our true home.

The premature strike at independence is over.
Jesus is too young now to cut the apron strings.
Parental hold is reestablished and accepted.
He will go home with them and be a good boy
And not worry them like that any more.
But they are on notice.
The conflict is not really resolved.
It is held in abeyance until the proper time should come.
Mary, mother that she was,
Kept careful memory of everything he said.

Some day the man would make it clear
What the boy had said and done.

Jesus had a streak of unpredictability,
Unless you knew the predictability of religious identity
Which takes precedence over social and familial claims.
He had a streak of independence, however obedient,
That would make him hard to manage and direct.
Nowadays we would call him a nonconformist.
He had a mind of his own,
A life of his own to live,
A consciousness of his own
To develop into a vocation of his own
Which parents could not share but only look after.

He was on his way.
He would be a man.
He would be what he already was:
The Son of God.

What that meant for him to do
Would be revealed in time.
When the time came,
He would be ready for it.

ON TURNING WATER INTO WINE

EPIPHANY II
John 2:1–11

WHOEVER says that water
    Can't be turned into wine
Has never been to a wedding.

Water would not turn into wine
Left simply by itself in large jars.
It requires a special occasion,
A particular Presence acting as agent.

Turning water into wine is God's thing.
He does it all the time
By very complicated processes,
All quite naturally.
What is wine but water
Stored up in grapes,
Juiced up for special occasions?

Wine is for celebration
At weddings and other times

When life is transformed
From ordinariness to beauty.

Just think of trying
To drink a toast to a young couple
With ordinary water.
Or try a Holy Communion
With bread and water.
Water is a beautiful liquid,
And ordinarily it tastes very good,
And nothing quenches thirst quite like it.
But it belongs to the ordinariness of life,
Not quite the thing, untransformed,
With which to celebrate life's magic moments.

Nor is wine for quenching thirst,
Any more than water's for toasts,
Or weddings for merely pairing off
Boys and girls.

Everybody dresses up for weddings.
If an ordinary girl can become a beautiful bride
And her young man a polished groom—
Neither seen in public quite like that before—
Think it not strange
That water should turn into wine in delight,

When Jesus is present for the occasion.
Even wine can change in other circumstance,
Taking on his blood for us in Holy Eucharist.

Whoever says that water
Can't be turned into wine
Has never been to a wedding.
Whoever says that wine
Cannot bring Jesus to us
Has never been to Holy Communion.
Whoever doubts these things
Has a lot to learn about Jesus,
God, and Spirit.

There is a chemistry
Which is not explained
In scientific laboratories.
It happens when God is present
To transform ordinariness
Into something very extraordinary.
Whoever doubts this miracle
Will live a whole life through
Without ever experiencing it,
Having nothing to celebrate
And nothing to celebrate with,

Except untransformed bread and water
For wine and cake and love and joy and Jesus.
"Wine makes glad the heart," the psalmist said.
An unbelieving soul (incredibly dour)
Would swear all wine was merely colored water
And never drink to taste the difference.
An Epiphany, of sorts, is needed for Eucharist.

A HEALING PRESENCE

EPIPHANY III
Matthew 8:1–13

A CENTURION requested Jesus to heal his servant.
Just a word would do it, the soldier said.
Military commands are to be carried out without question
In a system where everyone is under authority.
That the military should recognize spiritual authority
As superior is itself some kind of wonder.
Jesus calls that kind of faith
Greater than he had seen in all of Israel.
Jesus healed the sick servant at a distance.
The mere command was itself an impressive display of authority.

Let no one therefore make of faith a military virtue,
As if unquestioning obedience to God and man were its essence.
Jesus is not commander-in-chief of unquestioning disciples.
His disciples asked questions all the time
Without posing any threat to his authority.
It was the enemy he commanded with mere words
To let his people go. Demons, leprosy, disease, crippling,
Mysterious illnesses fled before him at mere command.
But he coerced no one into faith and commanded no allegiance.
He won his way into the hearts of men by freeing them.

Those who contested his authority were not subdued.
He simply exposed them for what they were.
No more could men dominate others in the name of religion
Without meeting Jesus' challenge.
Jesus' realm is freedom and his disciples ask questions.
His authority is that of a physician:
Death on germs for health of people,
Death on sin for saving people,
Death on demons for sanity of people,
Death on hypocrisy for souls of people.

The centurion did not know all the nuances of power.
He simply recognized authority when he saw it.
A man of war, his aim was the welfare of his men.

Furthermore, he recognized the limits of his authority.
He could command armies and put down rebellions,
But no disease of body or soul would flee at his command.
Military commanders are helpless before invaders
Who ravage men with mysterious illnesses.
What can a general do about infectious hepatitis,
Spinal meningitis, or psychotic stress?
War against disease requires authority of another kind.

We would do well to mark the difference.
What the military can do to cure man's ills is nil.
Often they destroy a place to save it.
This may be military logic, but it makes no human sense.
Healers have a different art from that of military strategy.
Surgeons make incisions, but not with swords.
Doctors give orders, but not for artillery strikes.
Psychiatrists probe men's minds, but not with hand grenades.

The Word works without hardware.
It makes its point and finds its target.
Christ's disciples are free people,
Not obedient soldiers under arms.
Let soldiers prate about how
They face the enemy with guns in hand,
Neglecting to mention "softening up" processes

Of aerial, naval, and artillery bombardment,
The air above layered thick with mobile ordinance.

Of course, it's gut-level reaction to come under enemy fire,
To be shot at in war, even with superior fire power on our side.
Bravery, besides guns, however many, still is needed.
We need not demean human courage or actuality of conflict
To say it is not enough to be obedient and brave
In a senseless, unjust, murderous cause.
Military duty does not exculpate man from human responsibility.

There are other kinds of courage.
Those who seek peace are not cowards.
Try going in sometime without the guns.
Try a bare head against police clubs,
Or a defenseless body against bullets which outrun protestors.
Try being an unarmed civilian caught in the cross fire.
Then shrug it all off, saying, "War is hell."

The centurion respects authority, blind obedience.
But he asks Jesus (does not command but asks respectfully)
To give a command he himself cannot issue
Against an enemy with which he cannot deal.
Still another centurion (or the same?),
When ordered to nail this same Jesus to a cross,
Will do it, because he is only following orders.

Sometime, somewhere, somehow, men will have to resist orders
Instead of obeying them and call murderous authority into question.
Such faith may not have been seen in all of Israel
But such stupidity has been seen everywhere in history.
Nor are we free from it; indeed, it increases daily.
When omnipotent militarists are stricken, however,
Or their servants, there is nothing to do
But call the medics and physicians.
Healing is not among the warrior's arts.
War can only kill.

When Jesus came, he healed without discrimination.
Sick and wounded soldiers are men, too,
Hurt, perhaps, more than most, and scarred for life.
A military man should shrink from nailing a healer to the cross,
No matter who commands.
For who shall heal the wounder
When the healer's dead?

There is an authority
To which captains and generals must yield.
All rulers, too, eventually.
They might even learn from it.
God shows *his* power
Chiefly by showing mercy.

CALMING STORMS

EPIPHANY IV
Matthew 8:23–27

ANOTHER thing Jesus does is calm storms.
But not right away.

There isn't a storm in human life God hasn't slept through.
He's a very hard sleeper, almost impossible to wake,
As everybody knows who tries to waken him with prayers.
We all talk bravely when we sit around in safety.
But when the storm comes, we're cowards every one.
We all pray hard during all the storms of life.

When the earth begins to quake beneath our feet,
When the savage sea begins to batter our small boats,
When clear-air turbulence begins to shake our plane apart,
It is no small panic which overcomes us.

God sleeps through it all.
Always he sleeps through it all.

Of course, we do not come running to him right away.
We let him sleep and don't bother him with prayers.
At the beginning, we think we can handle things by ourselves.

In fact, we like storms. They fascinate and excite us.
We love the agitation, the power, the chaos.
We love to experience it at the edge of danger.
We don't want to get caught up in it and become its victims.

We don't ask God if we should get into war or not.
We just get into it, like some wading pool
Which turns out to be quicksand. When tornadoes come,
We've been known to go out and look at them.
Some have even gone to the beach to watch tidal waves come in.
Homo sapiens is not always as bright as we like to think.

Jesus starts not with the storm but with us:
"Why are you so fearful, O ye of little faith?"
He's like some psychiatrist who tries to calm our anxieties,
As if the problem were all inward and there were no outside causes.
The problem is not our faith, it's the storm, we'd like to say.
But a crisis is no time to argue theology with God.
Let him have his say. There is a time
To talk about the nature and function of faith.
After the storm is past and we are safe we can talk about that.
Right now the important thing is to get God to do something.

Just because God sleeps it does not mean he is dead.
But we must admit, sometimes he is very hard to wake.

W E all know what Jesus is talking about.
He is not talking about wheat and tares but people.

We have all sorts of proverbs which deal with this situation.
"A rotten apple spoils the whole barrel."
One of our vice-presidents said
That we should separate dissenters from good people
With no more regret than we would have
In discarding rotten apples from the barrel.
That may not be what the kingdom of heaven is like,
But that's how we run things on earth.

If Jesus' view prevailed,
Common criminals would be let loose in society,
Unrestrained to do their damage
Instead of being in jail where they belong.
Preventive detention can solve a lot of problems in advance.
Outside agitators like Jesus could come into communities
And start trouble where only peace had prevailed before.
Campus radicals could bait cops and rile up students
To rock-throwing riot until there's no choice
But to gun some down to show we mean business.
Almost everybody agrees that shooting students
Will teach them a lesson.
As in war, of course, some innocents get hurt.

DISCRIMINATION
AND
WEEDING OUT

EPIPHANY V
Matthew 13:24–30

82

"You can't make an omelet without breaking eggs."
One of our wise men coined that phrase.

If Jesus had his way
We'd all have to wait till Judgment Day
To find out who's good and who's evil.
With all due respect to the way God does things,
We do things differently and more efficiently.

We're pretty good at weeding out.
We've got courts and prisons to take care of that.
People's rights have to come ahead of criminals' rights.
Individual rights must be weighed against society's needs.
Nor was the Inquisition such a bad idea.
We have information forms and dossiers,
Photographs and such, detection devices, neighbors' opinions,
All kinds of records going into master computer banks
To take care of disloyalists and other undesirables.
They may not be in jail where they belong,
But we can weed them out of jobs so they cannot live.

The kingdom of heaven, as Jesus describes it,
Is a very strange place. God has strange ideas.
Perhaps that's why Jesus got crucified, associating with sinners.
"Birds of a feather flock together."
"Where there's smoke, there's fire."

METAMORPHOSIS

THE TRANSFIGURATION OF OUR LORD
Matthew 17:1–9

WHEN God created man,
    It was a very significant event.
It was not yet very public.
Other animals watched
To see how this one would turn out.
To say that man was more than an animal
Would have confused them, perhaps,
For "human" did not belong to their vocabulary.
The setting for this silent experiment
Was in a garden of delight.

When God became a man,
The setting was not much different.
Animals were watching again.
This time a father and mother were present.
But that is no more than usual.
It took a while to discover
That Jesus was more than man was yet.

When God transfigured man,
It happened on a mountain
Far from the madding crowd.
It was also not a public event.
Even Jesus' closest friends
Didn't know exactly what was happening.
It would take a long time
For the significance of this event
To dawn on people.

First God made man.
Then God became man.
Then man became God.

The Son of God became the son of man
That the sons of men might become sons of God.
It is a rather remarkable metamorphosis.

Church fathers sensed it first:
"God became man that man might become God."
The nature of man is human.
His destiny is to become divine.

In Jesus God transfigured man.
Your turn is next.